**TWO OCEANS
PUBLISHING**

Published by Two Oceans Publishing

PO Box 1718
West Perth
WA 6872
Australia

ISBN 978-0-9943766-2-6

www.TwoOceansPublishing.com.au

Gut-Busting Jokes
for Kids

Compiled by Harriet Shaw

**TWO OCEANS
PUBLISHING**

2015

Gut Busting Jokes for Kids

What did the triangle say to the circle?

You're pointless.

How do you make a tissue dance?

Put a little boogey in it.

What did the pencil say to the other pencil?

You're looking sharp.

Why is basketball such a messy sport?

Because you dribble on the floor.

What has four wheels and flies?

A garbage truck.

What gets wetter the more it dries?

A towel.

Why do fish live in salt water?

Because pepper makes them sneeze.

What is the tallest building in the world?

The library. It has the most stories.

A man walking down the street sees a lady strolling along with a very big dog.

'Does your dog bite?' asks the man.

'No, he doesn't,' the lady replied.

The man pats the dog and has his hand bitten clean off.

'I thought you said your dog didn't bite,' moaned the injured man.

'That's not my dog,' replied the lady.

Two hikers were walking through the woods when they noticed a huge bear charging towards them in the distance. The first hiker removed his trail boots and began to lace up his running shoes. The second hiker laughed and said, 'Why bother changing out of your boots? You can't outrun a bear.' The first hiker replied, 'I don't have to outrun the bear, I only have to outrun you.'

What washes up on very small beaches?

Microwaves.

Why is a math book always unhappy?

Because it has lots of problems.

Why did the belt go to jail?

Because it held up a pair of pants.

What kind of key opens a banana?

A monkey.

When do you stop at green and go at red?

When you're eating a watermelon.

Why were the teacher's eyes crossed?

She couldn't control her pupils.

When is the best time to go to the dentist?

Tooth-hurty.

Why can you never trust atoms?

They make up everything.

What's the difference between a cat and a frog?

A cat has nine lives but a frog croaks every night.

What's the difference between a cat and a frog?

Why did the picture go to jail?

Because it was framed.

What do you give a dog with a fever?

Mustard, it's the best thing for a hot dog.

Why can't your nose be 12 inches long?

Because then it would be a foot.

Did you hear the joke about the roof?

Never mind, it's over your head.

Why did Sam go out with a prune?

Because he couldn't find a date.

Why do golfers wear two pairs of pants?

In case they get a hole in one.

What do you get when you cross fish and elephants?

Swimming trunks.

What do you give a lemon in distress?

Lemonade.

Where do you put barking dogs?

In a barking lot.

What kind of shoes do frogs wear?

Open toad.

What do you get when you cross a cheetah and a pie?

Fast food.

Knock knock.

Who's there?

Lettuce.

Lettuce who?

Let us in, we're freezing!

Knock knock.

Who's there?

Tank.

Tank who?

You're welcome!

Knock knock.

Who's there?

Adore.

Adore who?

Adore is between us – open up!

Knock knock.

Who's there?

Cash.

Cash who?

No thanks, but I'd love a peanut!

Knock knock.

Who's there?

Goat.

Goat who?

Go to the door and find out!

Knock knock.

Who's there?

Anita.

Anita who?

Anita borrow some money.

A man goes to the vet about his dog's fleas. The vet says, 'I'm sorry, but I'll have to put this dog down.' The man can't believe it and asks why, and the vet says, 'Because he is far too heavy.'

A man driving into town spots a truck broken down on the side of the road. He stops to help. The truck driver says he is on his way to deliver some penguins to the zoo. The truck driver says, 'I'll give you some cash if you could take the penguins to the zoo for me.' The man agrees. Later, when the truck is fixed, the truck driver drives into town and spots the man walking with a row of pengiuns waddling behind him, away from the zoo. The truck driver stops and yells, 'What are you doing? I gave you money to take the penguins to the zoo?' The man replies, 'I did, but we got change so now we're going to the movies!'

How do you make a fire with two sticks?

Make sure one's a match!

What does a clock do when it's hungry?

Goes back 4 seconds!

Why did the chicken go to jail?

Because he was using fowl language!

Which is faster, heat or cold?

Heat, because you can catch a cold!

What do you call a fish with no eye?

A fsh.

What did the paper clip say to the magnet?

I find you very attractive.

What do you get when you cross a teacher
with a vampire?

Lots of blood tests.

Why do birds fly south for the winter?

Because it's too far to walk.

What's a cat's favourite nursery rhyme?

Three blind mice.

What did the ocean say to the beach?

Nothing, it just waved.

What's bigger than an elephant, but doesn't weigh anything?

His shadow.

How long did Cain hate his brother?

As long as he was able.

Patient: 'Doctor, Doctor I think I'm a pair
of curtains.'
Doctor: 'Pull yourself together, man.'

Little Jimmy was visiting his grandfather. In the morning, his Grandpa decided to make oatmeal for breakfast and put some in a bowl for Jimmy.

'Do you like sugar?' he asked.

'Yes,' said Jimmy. So Grandpa put some sugar on the oatmeal.

'Do you like milk?'

'Yes,' said Jimmy. So Grandpa put some milk on the oatmeal.

'Do you like butter?'

'Yes,' said Jimmy.

So Grandpa put butter on the oatmeal and gave the bowl to Jimmy, who tasted it and said, *'Yukk!'*

'What's the matter? I asked you if you like sugar, milk, and butter and you said yes,' said Grandpa, getting angry.

'You didn't ask me if I like oatmeal,' said Jimmy.

A guy runs home and bursts in yelling with excitement, 'Pack your bags sweetheart, I've just won the lottery!' She goes, 'Hooray! Now should I pack for the beach or for the mountains?' He replies, 'I don't care . . . just pack and shove off!'

Sherlock Holmes and Dr Watson decide to go camping. They pitch their tent under the stars and go to sleep. In the middle of the night Holmes wakes Watson up.

'Watson, look up and tell me what you see.' Watson looks up and says, 'I see millions and millions of stars.' Holmes: 'And from that you deduce what?' Watson: 'Well, there are millions of stars, and if even a few of those have planets, it's quite likely there are some planets like earth out there. And if there are a few planets like earth out there, there might also be life.' Holmes: 'Watson, you idiot, somebody stole our tent.'

Why is wind energy so popular?

Because it has lots of fans.

Why couldn't the kid see the pirate movie?

It was rated arrr!

Why was the boy sitting on his watch?

He wanted to be on time.

What animal can jump higher than a house?

Any animal — houses can't jump.

How do baseball players stay cool?

They sit next to their fans.

Why was the student's report card wet?

It was below C level.

Why did the robber take a bath?

He wanted to make a clean getaway.

Why did the boy eat his homework?

His teacher said it was a piece of cake.

How many cops does it take to
change a light bulb?

None. It turned itself in.

How many opera singers does it take to
change a light bulb?

*One. They hold the bulb and the world
revolves around them.*

How many mystery writers does it take to
change a light bulb?

*Two. One to screw it almost all the way in and the
other to give it a surprising twist at the end.*

How many Mexicans does it take to change a light bulb?

Just Juan.

How many SAS men does it take to change a light bulb?

Three. One to change it and two to shout Go! Go! Go!

How many dogs does it take to change a light bulb?

Two. One to change it, and one to sniff the first one's butt.

Knock knock.

Who's there?

Wet.

Wet who?

Wet me in, it's raining out here.

Knock knock.

Who's there?

Dewey.

Dewey who?

Do we have to go to school today?

Knock knock.

Who's there?

Alison.

Alison who?

Alice in Wonderland.

Knock knock.

Who's there?

Arthur.

Arthur who?

Arthur any more chocolates left?

Knock knock.

Who's there?

Boo.

Boo who?

What are you crying about?

Knock knock.

Who's there?

Canoe.

Canoe who?

Canoe open the door please?

While robbing a home, a burglar hears someone say, 'Jesus is watching you.' To his relief, he realizes it is just a parrot mimicking something it had heard. The burglar asks the parrot, 'What's your name?' The parrot says, 'Moses.' The burglar goes on to ask, 'What kind of a person names their parrot Moses?' The parrot replies, 'The same kind of person that names his rottweiler Jesus.'

A big guy walks into a crowded bar and yells out: 'Is there a man by the name of Murphy here?' A little fellow stands up and says to him, 'I'm Murphy.' The big guy grabs him and starts beating him up. He cracks five of his ribs, breaks his nose, and gives him two black eyes. Then he flings him down on the floor and stomps out. After he's gone, the little fellow props himself up, saying softly, 'I sure made a fool of that guy. I'm not Murphy! Ha ha!'

There were two cows in a field. One said 'Moo' and the other one said 'Hey, I was going to say that!'

A little boy went up to his father and asks: 'Dad, where did all of my intelligence come from?' The father looks at his son and replies: 'Well, son, you must have gotten it from your mother, because I still have mine.'

The policeman rang the doorbell, unsure of how he was going to break the sad news. The door opened and a woman stood there gazing anxiously into the policeman's eyes.

'I'm sorry to inform you, Ma'am, but your husband's new watch is broken.'

'Broken?' she said, puzzled. 'How did that happen?' The policeman replied, 'A piano fell on him.'

Two boys were riding on a bicycle built for two. They had a very hard time going up a steep hill, but they finally got to the top.

'Whew,' said the first boy. 'I didn't think we'd ever make it.'

'Well, I helped,' said the second boy. 'I kept the brakes on so we wouldn't roll back down.'

A group of managers have been given the job of measuring the height of a flagpole. They go to the flagpole with a ladder and a measuring tape. They keep falling off the ladder, dropping the tape and the whole thing is a real mess. An engineer comes along and sees what they are trying to do. He walks over, pulls the flagpole out of the ground, lies it flat, measures it from end to end and gives the measurement to one of the managers. After he leaves, one manager turns to another and laughs. 'Isn't that just like an engineer? We are looking for the height and he gives us the length!'

Long ago, a sailing ship was in danger of being boarded by a pirate ship. As the crew became frantic, the captain bellowed to the first mate, 'Bring me my red shirt!' The first mate quickly retrieved the captain's red shirt, which the captain put on and led the crew to battle the pirate boarding party. Although some casualties occurred among the crew, the pirates were repelled. The men sat around on deck that night recovering and an ensign looked to the captain and asked, 'Sir, why did you call for your red shirt before the battle?' The captain replied, 'If I am wounded in battle the red shirt does not show blood, and thus you men will continue to fight unafraid.' The men sat in silence, marveling at the courage of such a man. The next morning, the lookout screamed that there were two pirate vessels sending boarding parties. The crew cowered in fear but the captain, calm as ever, bellowed, 'Bring me my red shirt!' Once again, the battle was on, and the captain and his crew repelled both boarding parties, though this time more casualties occurred. Later that day, however, the lookout screamed that there were pirate ships, ten of them, all with boarding parties on their way. The men became silent and looked to the captain, their brave leader, for his usual command. The captain, as calm as ever, bellowed, 'Bring me my brown trousers!'

Where do you keep a baby ape?

In an apricot.

What do you get when you pour boiling water
down a rabbit hole?

Hot cross bunnies.

What's the difference between a storm and a
lion with toothache?

One pours with rain and the other roars with pain.

What do you call a shoe made from a banana?

A slipper.

What do you call a gorilla with a banana in each ear?

Anything you like – he can't hear you.

What gives you the power to walk through a wall?

A door.

What do you call a teacher with no arms, no legs and no body?

The Head.

What are hippies?

They're what leggies hang from.

Why couldn't the bicycle stand up?

Because it was too tired.

What is brown and has a head and a tail but no legs?

A penny.

Why did the banana go to the Doctor?

Because it wasn't peeling well.

What stays in the corner and travels all over the world?

A stamp.

How do you drown a hipster?

In the mainstream.

What sound do porcupines make when they kiss?

Ouch!

What did the painter say to the wall?

One more crack like that and I'll plaster you!

Why couldn't the pirate play cards?

Because he was sitting on the deck.

A man goes to the doctor and says that every time he touches his foot he feels excruciating pain. The doctor notes it down and asks if it hurts anywhere else. To demonstrate, the man also touches his shin and thigh and screams out with pain. The doctor examines the man, but as he is unable to diagnose the source of the pain he refers him to a specialist. A few weeks later the man returns and the doctor eagerly asks the man if the specialist found out what was wrong. 'Yes,' said the man, 'he discovered my finger was broken!'

The teacher gave the little boy a problem. 'Now,' she said, 'if your father gave you ten cents and your mother gave you twelve cents, and then your uncle gave you fifteen cents more, what would you have?' The little boy immediately slipped into deep thought.

'Come on,' said the teacher, 'surely you can figure out a simple little problem like that.'

'It isn't a simple little problem,' the boy said. 'I can't decide whether I'd have a cream bun or a doughnut.'

A wife went to the police station with her neighbor to report that her husband was missing. The policeman asked her for a description. She said, 'He's 35 years old, 6 foot 4, has dark eyes, dark wavy hair, an athletic build, weighs 185 pounds, is soft-spoken and is good to the children.' The neighbor protested, 'Hang on, your husband is 5 foot 4 inches, chubby, bald, has a big mouth, and is mean to your children.' The wife replied, 'Yeah, but who wants *him* back?'

This woman rushes to her doctor, looking all strung out and very worried. She says to him: 'Doctor, take a look at me. When I woke up this morning I looked at myself in the mirror and saw that my hair was all wiry and frazzled up, my skin was all wrinkled and pasty, my eyes were bloodshot and bugging out, and I had this corpse-like look on my face! What's *wrong* with me, Doctor?' The doctor looks her over for a couple of minutes, then calmly says, 'Well, I can tell you there ain't nothing wrong with your eyesight . . .'

How many magicians does it take to change a light bulb?

That depends on what you want to change it into.

How many biologists does it take to change a light bulb?

Five. One to change it and four to write the environmental impact statement.

How many birds does it take to change a light bulb?

Toucan do it.

How many safety inspectors does it take to
change a light bulb?

*Four. One to change it and three to
hold the ladder.*

How many folk singers does it take to
change a light bulb?

*Five. One to change it, and four to sing about
how good the old one was.*

How many gorillas does it take to
change a light bulb?

One. But it takes a lot of bulbs.

A doctor says to his patient, 'Without this treatment you've only got 3 months to live,' and hands him a bill. The patient says, 'My God! Look at all these. I can't come up with this kind of money in 3 months!' The doctor says, 'Alright! You've got 6 months to live.'

A man runs into his house breathless and says to his wife, 'Honey, you should be proud of me, I just saved $2 by not taking the bus, but I chased it all the way home.' The wife replies, 'You want a medal for that? You should have chased a cab and saved yourself $15!'

A turtle was walking down an alley in New York when he was mugged by a gang of snails. A police detective came to investigate and asked the turtle if he could explain what happened. The turtle looked at the detective with a confused look on his face and replied, 'I don't know, it all happened so fast.'

A man walks into a bar and is about to order a drink when he notices Van Gogh playing the guitar in the corner. He calls over, 'Hey, Van Gogh! Want a drink?' Van Gogh replies, 'No thanks. I've got one 'ere.'

This chap lives alone so he went to the pet shop to get something to keep him company. The owner suggested a talking millipede.

'Okay,' he thought, a bit skeptically, 'I'll give it a go.' So he bought one, took it home and put it in a cardboard box. That evening he leaned over the box and said: 'I'm going to the pub for a drink, do you want to come?' There was no reply. He tried again, 'Hey there, millipede, wanna come to the boozer with me?' Again, there was no response. Disgusted by his gullible nature, he decided to give it one more try before returning the millipede to the pet shop.

'I said I'm going to the pub for a drink. Do you wanna come?'

'I heard you the first time!!' snapped the millipede, 'I'm just putting my flippin' shoes on . . .'

A man gets knocked down by a truck. A guy says to him, 'Are you comfortable.' He says, 'I make a living!'

The doctor says to the patient, 'You're in great health – you'll live to be 90.' The patient replies, 'But Doctor, I am 90!' The doctor responds, 'Well, that's it, then.'

There was a knock on the door in the early hours. The man went downstairs, opened the door and a voice said, 'Will you give us a push, mate?' The man was very angry, saying that it was a ridiculous hour to be waking people up, shut the door and went back upstairs. When his wife asked who it was, he told her it was some nutter wanting a push. She said, 'You shouldn't have refused; don't you remember when we broke down and were glad of a push?' So he went downstairs again, opened the door and said, 'Okay mate, where are you?' And a voice said, 'Over here on the swings.'

A man walks into a café and notices two big pieces of beef nailed to the ceiling. He asks the waiter why they're up there. 'It's a competition. If you can climb up there and get those bits of meat down you'll get free food all day. But if you try and fail then you'll have to buy lunch for everyone in the cafe. Do you fancy having a go?' The man has a long, hard look at the ceiling before saying, 'No, I'll just have a sandwich thanks. The steaks are too high.'

A family of tortoises went into a cafe for some ice cream. They sat down and were about to start eating when father tortoise said, 'I think its going to rain, Junior, will you pop home and fetch my umberella?' So off went Junior for father's umbrella. Three days later he still hadn't returned.

'I think, dear,' said mother tortoise to father tortoise, 'that we had better eat Junior's ice cream before it melts.' And a voice from the door said, 'If you do that I won't go.'

Knock knock.

Who's there?

Water.

Water who?

Water you doing in my house?

Knock knock.

Who's there?

Ada.

Ada who?

Ada hot dog for lunch.

Knock knock.

Who's there?

Alpaca.

Alpaca who?

Alpaca da trunk, you packa da suitcase.

Knock knock.

Who's there?

Turnip.

Turnip who?

Turnip the volume, it's quiet in here.

Knock knock.

Who's there?

Alma.

Alma who?

Alma not going to tell you.

Knock knock.

Who's there?

Ice cream.

Ice cream who?

Ice cream if you don't let me in.

What did one elevator say to the other elevator?

I think I'm coming down with something.

What is the best day to go to the beach?

Sunday, of course.

Why did Johnny throw the clock out of the window?

He wanted to see time fly.

What did one candle say to the other candle?

I'm going out tonight.

Why did the traffic light turn red?

You would too if you had to change in the middle of the street.

What do you get when you cross a cow and a duck?

Milk and quackers.

How do you make holy water?

Boil the hell out of it.

How many books can you put in an empty box?

One. After that it's not empty.

Which weighs more, a ton of feathers or
a ton of bricks?

Neither, they both weigh a ton.

What dog keeps the best time?

A watch dog.

Why did the computer go to the doctor?

Because it had a virus.

Why should you take a pencil to bed?

To draw the curtains.

What starts with a P, ends with an E, and
has a million letters in it?

Post Office.

Why don't skeletons fight each other?

They don't have the guts.

What did the blanket say to the bed?

Don't worry, I've got you covered.

What bow can't be tied?

A rainbow.

What has one head, one foot and four legs?

A bed.

What kind of button won't unbutton?

A belly button.

What did the traffic light say to the car?

Don't look now, I'm changing.

What did the grape do when it got stepped on?

Nothing, it just let out a little wine.

What goes up when the rain comes down?

An umbrella.

What did the stamp say to the envelope?

Stick with me and we will go places.

Which month do soldiers hate most?

The month of March.

What kind of shoes do spies wear?

Sneakers.

A shipwreck survivor washes up on the beach of an island and is immediately surrounded by a group of native warriors.

'I'm done for,' the man cries in despair.

'No, you are not,' comes a booming voice from the heavens. 'Listen carefully, and do exactly as I say. Grab the spear from the one who is beside you and shove it through the heart of the chief.' The man does so, and the remainder of the band stare in disbelief.

'Now, what?' the man asks the heavens.

'Now, you are done for.'

As a funeral train passes by a golf course, a golfer on one of the greens stops and stands at attention with his hat held over his heart as the hearse goes by. Then he goes back to lining up his putt. His playing partner remarks how that was the nicest gesture he'd ever seen, to show such respect for the dead. The first golfer sinks his putt and says, 'Well, she was a good wife for sixteen years.'

Mary's husband Tom has been slipping
in and out of a coma for several months,
yet his faithful wife stays by his bedside day
and night. One night, Tom comes to and
motions for her to come closer. He says,
'Mary, you have been with me through all the
bad times. When I got fired, you were there
to support me. When my business failed, you
were there. When I got shot, you were by my
side. When we lost the house, you gave me
support. When my health started failing, you
were still by my side. You know what, Mary?'

'What dear?' she asked gently.

'I think you're bad luck.'

A man is looking down from a plane as it flies
over the Pacific Ocean. He turns to the lady
next to him and asks: 'That island down there.
Is it pronounced Hawaii or Havaii?' The
woman replies, 'Havaii.' The man says:
'Thank you.' The woman replies: 'You're
velcome!'

A man walks into a restaurant and growls at the maitre d', 'Do you serve crabs here?' The maitre d' responds, 'We serve anyone. Have a seat, sir.'

A scientist who thought he knew everything was going on a business trip. On the airplane, he sat next to a lady. He asked her, 'Do you want to play a game? I ask you a question and if you can't answer, you give me $5 and then you ask me a question and I give you $5 if I can't answer?' 'No!' 'How about if I can't answer, I give you $1000, but if you can't answer, you only have to give me $5?' 'No!' 'How about if I can't answer, I give you $2000?' 'OK' 'What is the top speed of an Indian fruit bat?' The lady gave him $5 and asked him, 'What has 15 legs going up a hill, 137 legs at the top, and 57 legs coming down?' The man nearly busted his brain thinking about it but eventually he gave up and gave the lady $2000. Then he asked, 'So, what is the answer?' The lady gave him $5.

A guy tries to enter a nightclub but is stopped at the door by the bouncer who tells him that he can't get in without wearing a necktie. The guy goes back to his car, looks around but can't find a tie. He sees a set of jumper leads in the back so he puts them around his neck and ties a rough knot. He walks back to the nightclub. When the bouncer sees him he looks him over and says, 'Okay, you can go in – but don't start anything.'

This guy is walking past a wooden fence. On the other side of the fence is a lunatic asylum. The inmates are all screaming at the tops of their lungs, 'Thirteen! Thirteen! *Thirteen!!*' The guy notices a small hole in the fence and his curiosity naturally gets the better of him. He takes a peek and a finger suddenly pops out and jabs him in the eye. He yells in pain and the inmates start shouting, 'Fourteen! Fourteen! *Fourteen!!*'

How many politicians does it take to change a light bulb?

Two. One to change it, and one to change it back again.

How many monkeys does it take to change a light bulb?

Two. One to do it and one to scratch his bum.

How many drummers does it take to change a light bulb?

One . . . two, and a – one two three four . . .

How many Marxists does it take to
change a light bulb?

*None. The light bulb contains the seeds of
its own revolution.*

How many punk rockers does it take to
change a light bulb?

*Two. One to screw in the bulb and the other to
smash the old one on his forehead.*

How many philosophers does it take to
change a light bulb?

Hmm . . . that's an interesting question, isn't it?

What is the fastest way to determine the sex
of a chromosome?

Pull down its genes.

Mom: What did you learn in school?

Son: Not enough, I have to go back tomorrow.

What's ET short for?

Because he's got little legs.

If H_2O is water what is H_2O_4?

Drinking, bathing, washing, swimming . . .

What's the difference between a PhD in mathematics and a large pizza?

A large pizza can feed a family of four.

If school isn't a place to sleep then home isn't a place to study.

Patient: Doctor, people keep ignoring me.

Doctor: Next please.

If frozen water is iced water and frozen lemonade is iced lemonade, what's frozen ink?

Iced ink (I stink).

Where would you find a tortoise with no legs?

Wherever you left it.

What's red and looks like a bucket?

A red bucket.

How do hairdressers speed up their job?

They take short cuts.

What is a boxer's favourite drink?

Punch.

What do Mexicans keep under the carpet?

Underlay! Underlay! Underlay!

Why did the football coach go to the bank?

To get his quarterback.

What plant should you never invite on a boat trip?

A leek.

Why did the girl give her pony cough syrup?

Because it was a little horse.

Which side of a chicken has more feathers?

The outside.

What happens if a red ship crashes into a blue ship?

The crew gets marooned.

What's the difference between illegal and unlawful?

One is against the law and the other is a sick bird.

Why was the Egyptian girl worried?

Because her daddy was a mummy.

When is a vet busiest?

When it's raining cats and dogs.

What do you get if you lie face down under a cow?

A pat on the back.

Why did the man put his money in the freezer?

Because he wanted cold, hard cash.

What did one plate say to the other plate?

Dinner's on me tonight.

Knock knock.

Who's there?

Figs.

Figs who?

Figs the doorbell, it's broken.

Knock knock.

Who's there?

Howard.

Howard who?

Howard I know?

Knock knock.

Who's there?

Leaf.

Leaf who?

Leaf me alone.

Knock knock.

Who's there?

Amarillo.

Amarillo who?

Amarillo nice guy!

Knock knock.

Who's there?

Cow-go.

Cow-go who?

No, Cow-go moo.

Knock knock.

Who's there?

Yukon.

Yukon who?

Yukon say that again!

Knock knock.

Who's there?

Orange.

Orange who?

Orange you going to let me in?

Knock knock.

Who's there?

Amy.

Amy who?

Amy 'fraid I've forgotten?

Knock knock.

Who's there?

Olive.

Olive who?

Olive right next door to you.

A man is sat at home watching TV when he hears a knock at the door. The man gets up and answers the door, and to his astonishment there is a snail at the door. The snail says, 'Can I sell you some double glazing.' To which the man replies, 'No' and kicks him down the street. Two weeks later there is another knock at the door. The man answers it and it is the snail again. The snail then says, 'What did you do that for then?'

A man took his dog to the vet. 'Sorry,' said the vet, 'but your dog is dead.' The distraught man asks the vet for a second opinion – the vet brings in the practice cat. The cat sniffs around – no response from the dog. The vet says, 'Sorry, but your dog is dead.' The man insists on a third opinion, so the vet brings in the practice labrador. The practice dog sniffs around – no response from the man's dog. Reluctantly the man accepts that his dog is dead. On the way out, the receptionist gives him a bill for $1000. 'Good grief, what is this for?' 'Well,' said the receptionist, 'it's $100 for the vet, $300 for the catscan and $600 for the lab report.'

A man driving on a highway is pulled over by a police officer. The officer asks, 'Did you know your wife and children fell out of your car a kilometre back?' A smile creeps onto the man's face and he exclaims, 'Thank God! I thought I was going deaf!'

A newly ordained priest is nervous about hearing confessions and asks an older priest to observe one of his sessions to give him some tips. After a few minutes of listening, the old priest suggests that they have a word. 'I've got a few suggestions for you,' he says. 'Try folding your arms over your chest and rub your chin with one hand.' The new priest tries this. 'Very good,' says his senior. 'Now try saying things like "I see, I understand" and "Yes, go on."' The younger priest practises these sayings, too. 'Well done,' says the older priest. 'Now don't you think that's better than slapping your knee and saying, "No way! What happened next?"'

A couple of New Jersey hunters are out in the woods when one of them falls to the ground. He doesn't seem to be breathing and his eyes are rolled back in his head. The other guy whips out his cell phone and calls 911. He gasps to the operator, 'My friend is dead! What can I do?' The operator, in a calm soothing voice says, 'Just take it easy. I can help you. First, let's make sure he's dead.' There is a silence, and then a shot is heard. The guy's voice comes back on the line. He says, 'Okay, now what?'

A worried man goes to see his priest. 'Father, I'm very worried. I think that my wife may be trying to poison me.' Said the priest: 'Hold on my son, let me talk to your wife. Come back and see me tomorrow and I should be able to give you some advice.' The following day the man comes back to his priest who tells him: 'Well my son, I have talked to your wife for nearly two hours. My advice to you is: take the poison.'

What has two legs but can't walk?

A pair of trousers.

What do you call a boomerang that won't come back?

A stick.

Why did the pony get detention?

Because he was horsing around.

What is Dracula's favourite fruit?

Nectarines.

How long are a giraffe's legs?

Long enough to reach the ground.

Why did the dog keep tripping?

Because he had two left feet.

Where can you always find a skunk?

In the dictionary.

What's the best way to talk to a crocodile?

From a distance.

What do you call a silly old man?

A fossil fool.

Why is the letter T like an island?

Because it is in wa__t__er.

How many birthdays does the average person have?

Only one.

Why didn't the skeleton go to the dance?

He had no body to go with.

What goes up, but never comes down?

Your age.

How do you cut a wave in half?

Use a sea saw.

What did zero say to eight?

Nice belt.

Why did the boy take a ruler to bed?

To see how long he slept.

There are basically three kinds of people in the world. Those who can count and those who can't.

Boy: You're stupid!

Girl: Do you know who I am?

Boy: No.

Girl: I'm the principal's daughter.

Boy: Do you know who I am?

Girl: No.

Boy: Good!

One day little Johnny went into school all puzzled. He said to his teacher, 'Miss, will I get into trouble for something I haven't done?' His teacher said, 'No, of course not, why do you ask?' Little Johnny said, 'Because I haven't done my homework.'

Little Freddy had just started school. When he returned home after the first day his mother asked him, 'So, Freddy, what did you learn at school today?' Freddy said, 'I learned to write.' His mother said, 'Oh, what did you write?' Freddy then replied, 'I don't know. I haven't learned to read yet.'

A boy was walking along with a box and he met his friend. 'Guess how many chickens I have in this box, and I'll give you both of them,' he said.

After everyone was in bed the telephone rang.
'Is this one one one one?'
'No, this is eleven eleven.'
'Are you sure this isn't one one one one?'
'Yes, I'm sure. This is eleven eleven.'
'Well, I'm sorry to have gotten you up.'
'That's all right. I had to get up anyway. The phone was ringing.'

All the kids were trying to impress Grandpa, who had come for a visit. Timmy boasted, 'I'm first in arithmetic, Grandpa.' Sally said she had come in first in the spelling bee. Grandpa asked little Billy, 'What are you first in, Billy?'

'Well, I'm the first one out the door when the bell rings.'

A boy was talking to his mother.

'Gee, Mom, I'm really glad you named me Albert.'

'Why?'

'Because that's what all the kids at school call me.'

A three legged dog walks into a saloon in the Wild West. The barman asks him what he wants. The dog replies, 'I'm looking for the man that shot my paw.'

A guy walks in to his psychiatrist's office and says, 'Doc, you've got to help me. One night I dream I'm a tepee and the next night I dream I'm a wigwam.' The doctor says, 'Relax, man, you're two tents'

Two guys were walking along the street and one of them says to the other: 'I've realized that my wife is an angel.'

'Mine isn't human, either,' replied the second guy.

The psychiatrist was asking questions to test his patient.

'Do you ever hear voices without knowing who is speaking or where the voices are coming from?'

'Yes, sir, I do.'

'And when does this occur?'

'When I answer the telephone.'

A linguistics professor was lecturing to his class.

'In English,' he said, 'a double negative forms a positive. In some languages, though, such as Russian, a double negative is still a negative. However, there is no language in which a double positive can form a negative.'
A voice from the back of the room piped up, 'Yeah, right.'

A man goes to the doctor and says: 'Doctor, it hurts when I do this,' and raises his arm. 'Well, don't do it then,' says the doctor.

A drunk enters a restaurant and asks the waiter: 'Did you see me come in the door, there?'
    'Yes I did, sir.'
    'Have you ever seen me before?'
    'No, I haven't.'
    'Then, how did you know it was me?'

A new teacher was trying to make use of her psychology courses. She started her class by saying, 'Everyone who thinks they're stupid, stand up!' After a few seconds, Little Johnny stood up. The teacher said, 'Do you think you're stupid, Johnny?' Little Johnny replied, 'No, ma'am, but I hate to see you standing there all by yourself.'

Two bugs go out to a concert. When it's over one says to the other: 'Shall we walk home or take a dog?'

When NASA started sending up astronauts, they quickly discovered that ballpoint pens would not work in zero gravity. To combat the problem, NASA scientists spent a decade and $2 billion to develop a pen that writes in zero gravity, upside down, underwater, on almost any surface including glass and at temperatures ranging from below freezing to 300C. The Russians used a pencil.

Where do guinea pigs go for holidays?
Hamster Dam.

What fish went to college?
The piano tuna.

How do you keep an idiot in suspense?
I'll tell you next week.

Who invented fractions?
Henry the Eighth.

Why can you never starve in the desert?

Because of all the sand which is there.

Why can you never starve in the desert?

Because of all the sand which is there.

What lies under the ocean and shakes?

A nervous wreck.

What's a good parting gift?

A comb.

Why do bees hum?

Because they don't know the words.

How do you stop a rhino from charging?

Take away its credit card.

What's brown and sounds like a bell?

Dung.

What did the policeman say to his belly?

You're under a vest.

What's black and white and eats like a horse?

A zebra.

How do you join the police force?

Handcuff them together.

What do you call a thief who fell in a cement mixer?

A hardened criminal.

What happened after the wheel was invented?

It caused a revolution.

Who was the fattest mummy ever?

Two ton Carmen.

Why can't two elephants swim at the same time?

They only have one pair of trunks.

Why did the koala fall out of the tree?

Because it was dead.

What do you call a dry parrot?

Polyunsaturated.

What do you call a fly without wings?

A walk.

Doctor . . . Doctor . . . I think I'm turning into a wasp.

Hmm, give me a buzz if it gets worse.

Doctor . . . Doctor . . . I think I've got an inferiority complex.

No, you really are inferior.

Doctor . . . Doctor . . . I got trampled by a load of cows.

So I herd.

Doctor . . . Doctor . . . there's a man to see you with a wooden leg named Kramer.

What's his other leg called?

Doctor . . . Doctor . . . thank goodness you're
here, I'm at death's door.

Don't worry, I'll pull you through.

Doctor . . . Doctor . . . I feel as sick
as a dog.

I'll make an appointment for you at the vet.

Doctor . . . Doctor . . . my snoring wakes me
up every night.

Sleep in another room; then you won't hear it.

Doctor . . . Doctor . . . I think I'm turning
into a bridge.

Really, what's come over you?

Knock knock.

Who's there?

Carter.

Carter who?

Carter stray dog – is it yours?

Knock knock.

Who's there?

Colin.

Colin who?

Colin round to see you.

Knock knock.

Who's there?

Butcher.

Butcher who?

Butcher said I could come and visit you.

Knock knock.

Who's there?

Orang.

Orang who?

Orang the doorbell but it's not working.

Knock knock.

Who's there?

Avenue.

Avenue who?

Avenue knocked on this door before?

Knock knock.

Who's there?

Icing.

Icing who?

Icing – you give me money.

Knock knock.

Who's there?

Wade.

Wade who?

Wade a minute – I'll check.

Knock knock.

Who's there?

Jaffa.

Jaffa who?

Jaffa keep me waiting?

Knock knock.

Who's there?

Walter.

Walter who?

Walter a strange thing to say!

What is the difference between ignorance, apathy, and ambivalence? I don't know and I don't care one way or the other.

A truckdriver saw a priest hitchhiking. He thought he would do a good turn and pulled the truck over.

'No problem, Father! I'll give you a lift. Climb in the truck.' The happy priest climbed into the passenger seat and the truck driver continued down the road. Suddenly the truck driver saw a lawyer walking down the road and instinctively he swerved to hit him. But he remembered there was a priest in the truck with him, so at the last minute he swerved back away, narrowly missing the lawyer. But even though he was sure he missed the lawyer he still heard a loud thump. He glanced in his mirrors and when he didn't see anything, he turned to the priest and said, 'I'm sorry Father. I almost hit that lawyer.'

'That's okay,' replied the priest. 'I got him with the door!'

A guy goes to the doctor and complains that no matter what he does he can't get the tune of 'Green, Green Grass of Home' out of his head. The doctor examines him and says that he's got Tom Jones Syndrome. The guys asks if it's common. The doctor replies: 'It's not unusual.'

A length of rope went into a bar, sat on a stool and ordered a beer. The bartender looked up and said, 'Sorry, but we don't serve ropes in here.' Dismayed and disappointed, the rope went out and then he got an idea. He stopped a man in the street and asked, 'Will you please tie a knot in me and separate my strands at both ends?' The man obliged, and with this done, the rope went back into the bar and once again ordered a beer. The bartender looked him over and said, 'Say, aren't you that same rope who was in here before?'

'No,' was the reply, 'I'm a frayed knot.'

Some tourists in the Museum of Natural History were marveling at the dinosaur bones. One of them asked the guard, 'Can you tell me how old the dinosaur bones are?' The guard replied, 'They are 3 million, four years, and six months old.'

'That's an awfully exact number,' says the tourist. 'How do you know their age so precisely?' The guard answered, 'Well, the dinosaur bones were three million years old when I started working here, and that was four and a half years ago.'

A man is walking down the street carrying a rabbit. Another man meets him.

'How much goes this donkey cost?' the second man asks.

'It's not a donkey, it's a rabbit,' the first man replies.

'I didn't ask you,' the second man says, 'I'm asking the rabbit!'

An insurance investigator is at a wedding reception, and asks the bride, 'So this is your fourth husband?'

'Yes, that's right,' she replied.

'Can I ask what happened to your first husband?'

'Oh, it's very sad, he died quite suddenly.'

'Oh, I am sorry, what happened?'

'Unfortunately he ate some poisoned mushrooms and passed away. The insurance paid out, of course, but it can never really compensate.'

'That's terrible, what happened to your second husband?'

'Another tragic case. He too, ate some poisoned mushrooms and passed away. The money didn't compensate for his loss either.' By now, the investigator was very suspicious, and asked; 'Did your third husband die from ingesting poisoned mushrooms?'

'Oh no no,' she stated, 'He died from a fractured skull!'

'My word, I am *very* sorry to hear that. How did that happen?'

'Well, he wouldn't eat the mushrooms!'

Why does your teacher have her hair in a bun?

Because she has a face like a burger.

What do sea monsters eat?

Fish and ships.

How do you know if there's an alien in your house?

There's a spaceship parked in your garden.

Where's the best place to keep a pie?

In your tummy.

Why do cows have bells?
Because their horns don't work.

What do you call a deer with no eyes?
No idea.

What do you call an Italian with a rubber toes?
Roberto.

What has more courage, a stump or a rock?
A rock, because it's a little boulder.

What do you get if you cross a pig and a laundry?

Hogwash.

Why do gorillas have big nostrils?

Because they've got big fingers.

How do you get eggs without chickens?

By keeping geese and ducks.

What's yellow and stupid?

Thick custard.

Why did the man have a sausage behind his ear?

He'd just eaten his pencil.

Why can't cheetahs play hide and seek?

Because they are always spotted.

Why is that man standing in the sink?

He's a tap dancer.

What's the leading cause of dry skin?

Towels.

Knock knock.

Who's there?

Othello.

Othello who?

Othello could freeze to death out here.

Knock knock.

Who's there?

Canoe.

Canoe who?

Canoe help me with my homework, please?

Knock knock.

Who's there?

Europe.

Europe who?

Europe bright and early today.

Knock knock.

Who's there?

Kong.

Kong who?

Kongratulations, you've won the lottery.

Knock knock.

Who's there?

Nana.

Nana who?

Nana your business.

Knock knock.

Who's there?

Karl.

Karl who?

Karl again another day.

Knock knock.

Who's there?

Jerome.

Jerome who?

Jerome at last.

Knock knock.

Who's there?

Pecan.

Pecan who?

Pecan someone your own size.

Knock knock.

Who's there?

Giselle.

Giselle who?

Giselle newspapers in there?

Knock knock.

Who's there?

Lass.

Lass who?

How long have you been a cowboy?

Knock knock.

Who's there?

Who.

Who who?

Is there an owl in here?

Knock knock.

Who's there?

Bart.

Bart who?

Bart time you opened the door.

A man was sitting on a bench by the beach eating some fish and chips when a little dog came along and started chewing hungrily at his trouser leg. The man looked at the dog's owner, who was doing nothing about this, and asked him if it was all right to throw the dog a bit.

'Yes, of course you can throw him a bit,' replied the owner. So the man picked up the dog and threw it into the ocean.

Johnny: Hello, I'm home!

Mother: Why are you home from school so early?

Johnny: I was sent home because Freddy was smoking.

Mother: But if Freddy was smoking, why were *you* sent home?

Johnny: Because I was the one who set him on fire.

Two students and their teacher are walking around the back of their school and they find an old oil lamp lying near a rubbish bin. They rub the lamp and a genie comes out in a puff of smoke.

'I usually only grant three wishes,' the genie says to them. 'So I'll give each of you just one.'

'Me first! Me first!' says the student who had picked up the lamp. 'I want to be in the Bahamas, driving an incredible speedboat, with an unlimited supply of cookies and soft drink.' Poof! He's gone.

'Me next! Me next!' says the other student. 'I want to be in Hawaii, relaxing by the pool of a massive house with a burger in my hand and two Ferraris in the garage.' Poof! He's gone as well.

'Okay, you're next,' the Genie says to the teacher. The teacher says, 'I want those two back in class after lunch.'

Newspaper reports say a toilet's been stolen.
Police say they have nothing to go on.

A husband stepped onto one of those penny scales that tell you your fortune and weight and dropped in a coin.

'Listen to this,' he said to his wife, showing her a small, white card. 'It says I'm energetic, bright, resourceful and a great person.'

'Yes,' his wife nodded, 'and it has your weight wrong, too.'

Mum: Come on, James, eat your breakfast; you`ll be late for school.

James: I don`t want to go to school. The teachers don't like me; the children don't like me – even the caretaker doesn't like me!

Mum: All the same, you have to go.

James: Why should I go?

Mum: Well, for one thing, you're forty-five years old, and for another you're the headmaster.

A man was walking in the country one day and he saw a pig with a wooden leg sitting outside a barn. As he was pondering this, the pig's owner came along. The man asked the farmer how the pig got his wooden leg. The farmer said, 'Let me tell you, sir, that is some pig! Our house caught fire last July and he dragged my kids to safety!'

'Wow! So is that how he lost his leg?' the man asked.

'No,' replied the farmer. 'But a month ago I almost drowned in the lake and that pig swam through icy water to pull me to shore!'

'Oh, so that's how he lost his leg,' the man said.

'Heck, no. And just about a week ago, my wife's car slid off the road onto the train tracks. That pig broke through the window and helped her out just as a freight train came through!'

'So *that's* how he lost his leg!' the man said.

'No, sir.'

'Then *how* did he lose it?' the man begged.

'Well, sir,' the farmer replied, 'when you got a pig that terrific, you don't want to eat it all at once.'

Famous last words

Listen, I know poison when I taste it.

Watch, I'll prove it.

Hey look, a light at the end of the tunnel.

I've seen this done on TV.

What does this button do?

Don't worry, we outnumber them.

This train track hasn't been used since 1947.

I drank what?

I think it's trying to communicate.

Don't worry – it's not loaded.

I can't believe no one has thought of this before.

They can't hit us at this range.

What do you call a man with leaves in his undies?

Russell.

What do you call a bag of parrot food?

Polly filla.

What do you call a small parent?

A minimum.

What do you call a chicken that eats cement?

A bricklayer.

What do you call a policeman with blond hair?

A fair cop.

What do you call a dog that's always fighting?

A boxer.

What do you call a fight between actors?

Star wars.

What do you call a dentist in the marines?

A drill sergeant.

What do you call a baby crab?

A nipper.

What do you call a cat that chases outlaws?

Posse.

What do you call a pig driving a car?

Road hog.

What do you call a man that can't swim?

Bob.

What do you call a man that steals things?

Rob.

What do you call a homeless snail?

A slug.

What do you call a vicar on a motorcycle?

Rev.

What do you call a smelly giant gorilla?

King pong.

What is smelly and has no sense of humour?

A dead hyena.

Did you hear the joke about the perfume?

I better not tell you – it stinks.

Where do sheep get their hair cut?

At the baa baa shop.

What do cows eat for breakfast?

Moosli.

What kind of person loves cocoa?

A coconut.

What did you hear of the farmer who won a Nobel prize?

He was out standing in his field.

Why did the man take his clock to the vet?

Because it had ticks.

What game do skunks play?

Ping pong.

What's bright blue and weighs five tons?

An elephant holding its breath.

Why did the projector blush?

Because it saw the film strip.

What grows down as it grows up?

A goose.

What do you get if you cross a mammal with a reptile?

A Nobel prize.

When do lions have eight feet?

When there are two of them.

What was the chicken doing on the runway?

Two miles an hour.

What goes ha ha ha bonk?

A man laughing his head off.

What do you call a pig that does karate?

A pork chop.

Which is the trendy horse?

The one with the pony tail.

How do you make a venetian blind?

Poke him in the eye.

What dies but never lives?

A battery.

Why aren't elephants allowed on the beach?

Because they can't keep their trunks up.

The old man had been a commuter on the train for decades. One day there was a new inspector, and he asked for the old fellow's ticket.

'My face is my ticket,' said the old boy.

'Well,' replied the inspector, taking off his jacket and rolling up his sleeves, 'I have orders to punch all tickets.'

A pirate walks into a pub. Another patron, having never met a pirate before, wants to know the stories behind the battle scars. He buys the pirate a drink and strikes up a conversation.

'How'd you get the peg leg?'

'Shark took off me leg in the South Seas.'

'How about that hook?'

'Lost the hand in a sword fight.'

'And the eye patch?'

'Seagull pooped in me eye.'

'Gosh, are seagull droppings really that dangerous?'

'No, but it were me first day with the hook.'

An Englishman touring the USA stopped in a remote bar in the hills of Nevada. He was chatting to the bartender when he spied an old Indian sitting in the corner.

'Who's he?' asked the Englishman.

'Oh, that's the Memory Man. He knows everything. He can remember any fact. Go and try him out.' So the Englishman goes over, and thinking he won't know anything about English football, asks 'Who won the 1965 FA Cup Final?'

'Liverpool,' replies the Memory Man.

'Who did they beat?'

'Leeds,' was the reply.

'And the score?'

'2-1.'

'Who scored the winning goal?'

'Ian St. John,' was the old man's reply. The Englishman was totally amazed by this and he told everyone about the Memory Man when he got back home. A few years later he went back to the USA and tried to find the Memory Man. Eventually he found the bar and sitting in the same seat was the old Indian. Because he was so impressed the Englishman decided to greet the Indian in his native tongue. He approached him with the greeting, 'How.' The Memory Man replied, 'Diving header in the six yard box.'

A group of kindergarten children were on a class outing to their local police station where they saw pictures, tacked to a bulletin board, of the ten most wanted men. One of the youngsters pointed to a picture and asked if it really was the photo of a wanted person.

'Yes,' answered the policeman.

'Well,' wondered the child, 'why didn't you keep him when you took his picture?'

A cross and hungry panda went into a bar and, without ordering a drink, demanded a bowl of free bar-snacks. The bartender refused, saying, 'Those snacks are for paying customers.' So the panda grabbed the nearest bowl and gobbled up all the snacks. Then he pulled out a revolver, shot the bartender dead, and stalked out. The customers all asked each other, 'Who was that masked maniac?' The quiet little guy at the end of the bar calmly answered, 'That was a panda. He eats shoots and leaves.'

Ted received a parrot for his birthday. The parrot was fully grown but it had a very bad attitude and worse vocabulary. Every other word was a swear word, and those that weren't swear word were, to say the least, rude. Ted tried to change the bird's attitude by always saying lots of polite words, playing soft music, anything he could think of. Nothing worked. He yelled at the bird and the bird got worse. He shook the bird and the bird got madder and more rude. Finally, in a moment of sheer desperation, Ted put the parrot in the freezer. For a few moments after he heard the bird swearing, squawking, kicking and screaming and then, suddenly, there was absolute quiet. Ted became frightened that he might have actually hurt the bird, and quickly opened the freezer door. The parrot calmly stepped out onto Ted's extended arm and said, 'I'm sorry that I have offended you with my language and my actions, and I ask your forgiveness. From this point forward I will endeavour to correct my behaviour.' Ted was astounded at the changes in the bird's attitude and was about to ask what had changed him, when the parrot continued, 'May I ask what the chicken did?'

Which monster is the best dance partner?

The boogie man.

What does a grape and an antelope have in common?

Neither of them can drive a tractor.

Why is Toblerone triangular?

So it will fit in the box.

What always succeeds?

A budgie without teeth.

What has four legs and flies?

Two pairs of trousers.

What's green and fluffy?

Green fluff.

What do you call an elephant in a phone booth?

Stuck.

What did the robot say to the petrol pump?

Take your finger out of your ear when I talk to you.

Why did the toilet paper roll down the hill?

It wanted to get to the bottom.

What's the best way to communicate with a fish?

Drop it a line.

Why are brides so unlucky?

They never marry the best man.

Where does an eight foot gorilla sleep?

Wherever it wants to.

When do you get that rundown feeling?

When a car hits you.

How do you catch a rabbit?

Hide behind a shrub and make a noise like a carrot.

What is grey and highly dangerous?

An elephant with a hand grenade.

What has a bottom at the top?

Your legs.

Waiter . . . Waiter . . . there's a fly in my soup.

*No, sir, that's a cockroach. The fly
is on your steak.*

Waiter . . . Waiter . . . do you have frog's legs?

No, sir, I've always walked this way.

Waiter . . . Waiter . . . this egg is bad.

Don't blame me, sir, I only laid the table.

Waiter . . . Waiter . . . there's a fly in my soup.

*Surely not, sir, it must be one of those vitamin
bees you hear so much about?*

Waiter . . . Waiter . . . there's a fly in my soup.

There couldn't be, sir. The chef used them all in the raisin bread.

Waiter . . . Waiter . . . there's a beetle in my soup.

Sorry, sir, we're out of flies today.

Waiter . . . Waiter . . . this bread tastes funny.

Then why aren't you laughing?

Waiter . . . Waiter . . . this coffee is terrible. It tastes like dirt.

Yes, sir, it was ground yesterday.

Waiter . . . Waiter . . . there's a fly in my soup.

*Don't worry, sir. The spider in your salad
will soon get him.*

Waiter . . . Waiter . . . there's a fly in my soup.

What do you expect for three dollars – a beetle?

Waiter . . . Waiter . . . your tie is in my soup.

Don't worry, it's not shrinkable.

Waiter . . . Waiter . . . what's this creepy crawly
thing doing in my dinner?

Oh, that one? He comes here every night.

A man walks into a butcher's shop and asks the butcher, 'Have you got a sheep's head?'

'No,' replies the butcher, 'it's just the way I part my hair.'

Two nuns were travelling through Europe in their car. They get to Transylvania and are stopped at a traffic light. Suddenly, a little vampire jumps onto the car and starts to scratch at the windshield!

'Quick, quick!' shouts the first nun, 'What shall I do?'

'Turn the windshield wipers on, that will get rid of the abomination,' shouts the second. The nun switches them on, knocking the vampire about, but he clings on and hisses even more loudly!

'What shall I do now?' shouts the first nun.

'Switch on the windshield washer. I filled it up with holy water in the Vatican!' says the second. The vampire steams as the water burns his skin but he clings on and hisses again at the nuns.

'Now what?' screams the first nun.

'Show him your cross!' says the second nun. So the nun rolls down the window and shouts: *'Get off my freakin' car you little jerk!'*

Did you hear about the ice-cream man found dead in his van, covered in chocolate sauce and hundreds-and-thousands? The police said he had topped himself.

A couple goes to a psychiatrist. The woman says, 'Doc, my husband thinks he's a dog. Can you help him?' The shrink says, 'Sure, have him lie down on the couch.' The woman says, 'Oh no. He's not allowed on the couch.'

One day little Johnny was in his back yard digging a hole. His neighbor, seeing him there, decided to investigate. 'Whatcha doing?' he asked. 'My goldfish died and I'm burying him,' Johnny replied. 'That's an awful big hole for a goldfish, ain't it?' asked the neighbor. 'That's because he's inside your cat!'

A flash flood swept over an area, stranding a man in his house. As the water rose, a rescue team came by in a boat.

'Get in,' the rescuers said. 'We'll take you to safety.'

'No,' said the man. 'I have faith in the Lord. He will save me.' The rains continued and the man was forced up onto his roof to avoid drowning. Soon, another boat came by.

'Sir, please get in,' the rescuers in this boat said. 'The waters are rising. We'll take you to safety.'

'No,' said the man again. 'I have faith in the Lord. He will save me.' The boat left, and soon the man was barely able to keep his head above water. The water became rougher and a helicopter was dispatched to save the man.

'We'll lower a rope. Get in the 'copter!' yelled the rescuers from above, 'The water shows no sign of abating. You're sure to drown!' Once again, the man refused.

'I have faith in the Lord,' he said calmly, 'He will save me.' Eventually, the man did, in fact, drown. When he got to heaven, he saw the Lord and approached him.

'What happened?' asked the man. 'I had faith that you would save me from drowning. Why didn't you?'

'Hey,' replied the Lord. 'I sent two boats and a helicopter. What else did you want?'

The End

Thank you for reading

Gut Busting Jokes for Kids

We hope you enjoyed it!

www.ingramcontent.com/pod-product-compliance
Lightning Source LLC
Chambersburg PA
CBHW021129020426
42331CB00005B/689